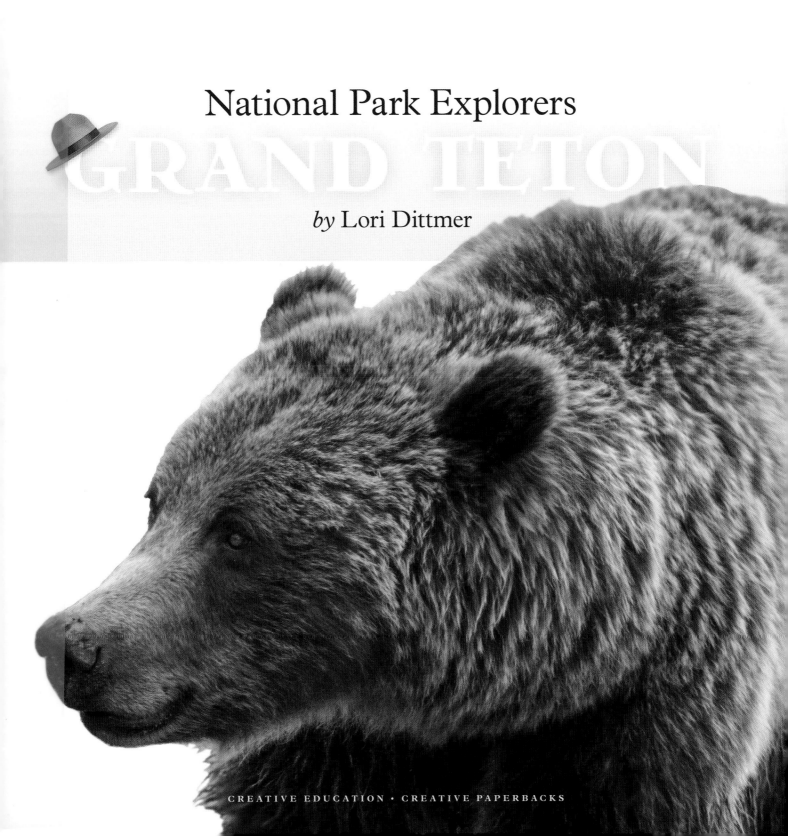

National Park Explorers

GRAND TETON

by Lori Dittmer

CREATIVE EDUCATION • CREATIVE PAPERBACKS

TABLE OF CONTENTS

A hot-air balloon is a fun way to see the Tetons.

WELCOME TO GRAND TETON NATIONAL PARK!

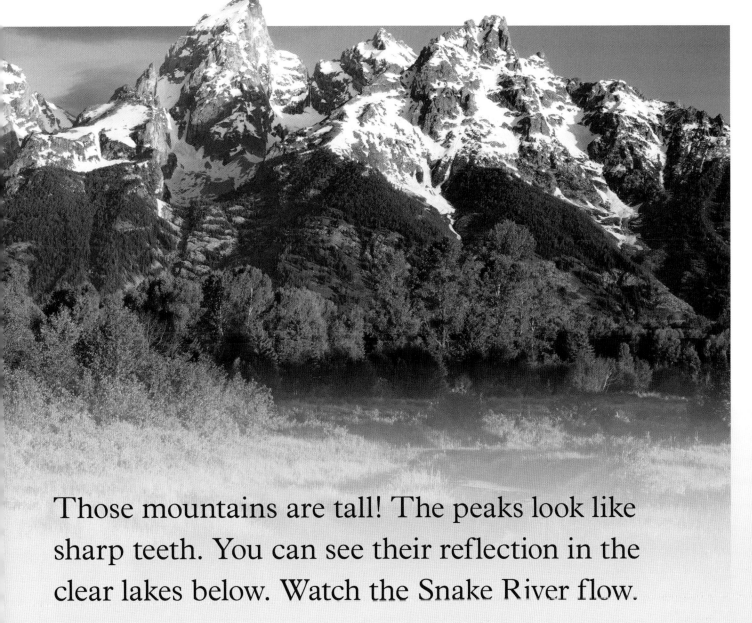

Those mountains are tall! The peaks look like sharp teeth. You can see their reflection in the clear lakes below. Watch the Snake River flow.

Grand Teton is the tallest mountain of the Tetons. This mountain range in Wyoming became a national park in 1929. In 1950, the valley of Jackson Hole was added to the park.

★ *Grand Teton National Park*
■ *Wyoming*

Grand Teton (above) is north of Jackson, Wyoming (right).

6

THE PARK'S FAULT

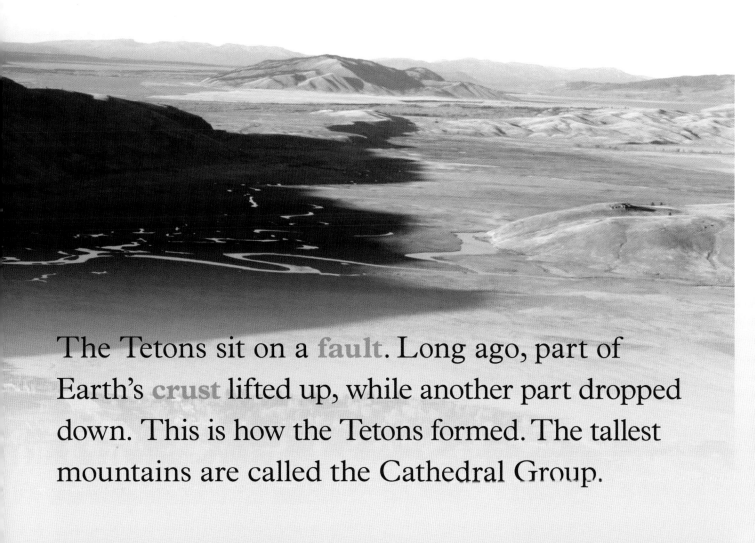

The Tetons sit on a fault. Long ago, part of Earth's crust lifted up, while another part dropped down. This is how the Tetons formed. The tallest mountains are called the Cathedral Group.

Glaciers can be found high in the Tetons. One of the largest is Skillet Glacier. It looks like a frying pan! Most of the glaciers are shrinking. Melted glaciers form cold ponds and lakes.

Skillet Glacier on Mt. Moran (below); Grand Teton range (right)

SIGNS OF LIFE

Leafy sagebrush carpets the valley. Forests of
conifers climb the mountainsides. Colorful
wildflowers bloom between May and September.

13

Wildlife is all around. Trout swim in the river. Trumpeter swans paddle on the water. Moose roam the woods. Bears look for food.

Trumpeter swans (below); a moose (right)

14

RECREATION EVERYWHERE

More than 4 million people visit Grand Teton each year. Many enjoy fly-fishing in the Snake River. Some go boating on Jenny Lake.

You can bike or drive through the park. Learn about early explorers at **historic** spots.

Buildings from the 1890s can be seen in the Jackson Hole area.

Skiers and campers love Grand Teton. They wear layers of clothing in case the weather changes. Climbers go up and down the mountains. Routes range from easy to extreme!

The park receives about 40 feet (12.2 m) of snow during an average winter.

Activity

MAKING SNOW

Materials needed:
1 cup baking soda
Bowl (or other container)
Shaving cream

Step 1: Put the baking soda in the bowl.

Step 2: Slowly mix in the shaving cream until you have a snow-like consistency.

Step 3: Make a snowball! This "snow" stays cool to the touch. Does it feel powdery? This is how real snow feels when it is really cold outside!

Glossary

conifers — trees or shrubs that produce cones and usually evergreen needles

crust — the outermost rock layer of the earth

fault — a place where sections of Earth's crust meet

glaciers — slow-moving masses of ice and snow

historic — important to the past

Read More

Gregory, Josh. *Grand Teton*. New York: Children's Press, 2018.

National Geographic Kids. *National Parks Guide USA Centennial Edition: The Most Amazing Sights, Scenes, and Cool Activities from Coast to Coast!* Washington, D.C.: National Geographic, 2016.

Websites

National Geographic Kids: National Parks
https://kids.nationalgeographic.com/explore/nature/national-parks/
Learn about the national parks of the United States, and take a quiz.

National Park Service: Grand Teton National Park for Kids
https://www.nps.gov/grte/learn/kidsyouth/index.htm
Find out how to become a junior ranger, and play online games.

Note: Every effort has been made to ensure that the websites listed above are suitable for children, that they have educational value, and that they contain no inappropriate material. However, because of the nature of the Internet, it is impossible to guarantee that these sites will remain active indefinitely or that their contents will not be altered.

Index

Published by Creative Education and Creative Paperbacks
P.O. Box 227, Mankato, Minnesota 56002
Creative Education and Creative Paperbacks are imprints of
The Creative Company
www.thecreativecompany.us

Design by Christine Vanderbeek
Production by Dana Cheit
Art direction by Rita Marshall
Printed in the United States of America

Photographs by Alamy (Photononstop, YAY Media AS), Creative
Commons Wikimedia (Acroterion), Dreamstime (Wisconsinart),
Getty Images (Kick Images), iStockphoto (Adventure_Photo,
AlexRaths, amygdala_imagery, AndrewSoundarajan, BWFolsom,
FRANKHILDEBRAND, gelyngfjell, Jeremy Hardin, joshbeckner,
juliannafunk, KenCanning, KevinCass, moose henderson,
mtruchon, PGile, RiverNorthPhotography, Ron_Thomas,
skibreck, YinYang), Shutterstock (Tarchyshnik Andrei, Dmitrij
Skorobogatov)

Library of Congress Cataloging-in-Publication Data
Names: Dittmer, Lori, author. • Title: Grand Teton / Lori Dittmer.
Series: National park explorers. • Includes bibliographical
references and index. • Summary: A young explorer's introduction
to Wyoming's Grand Teton National Park, covering its mountain
landscape, plants, animals such as moose, and activities such as fly
fishing. • Identifiers: ISBN 978-1-64026-067-2 (hardcover) / ISBN
978-1-62832-655-0 (pbk) / ISBN 978-1-64000-183-1 (eBook)
This title has been submitted for CIP processing under LCCN
2018938990.

CCSS: RI.1.1, 2, 3, 4, 5, 6, 7, 10; RI.2.1, 2, 3, 5, 6, 7; RI.3.1, 3, 5, 7;
RF.1.1, 3, 4; RF.2.4

First Edition HC 9 8 7 6 5 4 3 2 1
First Edition PBK 9 8 7 6 5 4 3 2 1